Nashwa Gaber

The Tomb of Ia-Maat in Saqqara

UNIVERSITY OF WARSAW • INSTITUTE OF ARCHAEOLOGY • DEPARTMENT OF ARCHAEOLOGY OF EGYPT & NUBIA

Warsaw 2013

Editor: Kamil O. Kuraszkiewicz
Drawings: Beata Błaszczuk
Photographs: Jarosław Dąbrowski
DTP: MOYO - Teresa Witkowska
Cover design: Teresa Witkowska and Kamil O. Kuraszkiewicz

Hieroglyphic inscriptions typeset with JSesh software by Serge Rosmorduc (jsesh.qenherkhopeshef.org).

ISBN 978-83-915941-6-2

„Pro-Egipt" Wydawnictwo Książkowe Andrzej Niwiński
ul. Zagłoby 35 m 1, 02-495 Warszawa
Wydanie I – Warszawa 2013
Nakład 150 egz.

druk:
Mazowieckie Centrum Poligrafii · 05-270 Marki ul. Duża 1 · www.c-p.com.pl

This book is dedicated to my Professor Zahi Hawass,
for his kindness, devotion, and his endless support.

ACKNOWLEDGEMENTS

I would like to express my special gratitude and appreciation to Prof. Karol Myśliwiec for his time, support and guidance. It was Professor Karol's attitude towards Ancient Egypt, which made me insist to complete this work.

I am deeply indebted to the following persons for their assistance during my studies and in preparing the present work: Dr. Tarek El Awady who helped me so much by spending with me many hours daily, discussing every detail of the text, Prof. Naguib Kanawati and Dr. Ramadan Hussein, whose important role and encouraging words will never be forgotten, as well as my dear Friends, Dr. Mohamed Ismail and Dr. Kamil Omar Kuraszkiewicz. Nothing could properly express my gratitude for their efforts.

Extremely helpful and generous in sharing their competence with me were also Beata Błaszczuk, Jarosław Dąbrowski, Marek Woźniak, Małgorzata Radomska – my genuine Polish sister, as well as Mr. Kamal Wahid, Mr. Saleh Atiya, Mr. Sabri Farag, Dr. Amal Samuel, Dr. Mohamed Megahed, Dr. Hana Vymazalova and Dr. Mahmoud Kassem.

I would like to express my appreciation and thanks to my husband Mostafa, my son Ahmed, my daughter Basant, my mother Sanaa, my brother Mohamed, and my sister Marwa. It was their enduring support and passion which made me able to finish this work.

Special thanks are accorded to Institutions which have made my studies in Poland possible: the Polish Centre of Mediterranean Archaeology and the Institute of Archaeology of the University of Warsaw, the Institute of Mediterranean and Oriental Cultures, Polish Academy of Sciences and – last but not least – the Polish Archaeological Mission in Saqqara.

CONTENTS:

ABBREVIATIONS AND BIBLIOGRAPHY

PERIODICALS AND SERIES

ASAE Annales du Service des Antiquités de l'Égypte, Cairo
BIFAO Bulletin de l'Institut Français d'Archéologie Orientale, Cairo
JEA Journal of Egyptian Archaeology, London
MDAIK Mitteilungen des Deutschen Archäologischen Instituts, Abteilung Kairo, Mainz

MONOGRAPHS

Abusir and Saqqara 2000
M. Bárta, J. Krejčí (eds.), *Abusir and Saqqara in the Year 2000, ArOr* Supplementa IX, Prague 2000.

Abusir and Saqqara 2005
M.Bárta, F. Coppens, J. Krejčí (eds.), *Abusir and Saqqara in the Year 2005*, Praha 2006.

Baer, *Rank and Title*
K. Baer, *Rank and Title in the Old Kingdom: The Structure of the Egyptian Administration in the Fifth and Sixth Dynasties*, Chicago 1960.

Barta, *Opferliste*
W. Barta, *Die altägyptische Opferliste, von der Frühzeit bis zur griechisch-römischen Epoche*, MÄS 3, 1963.

Bárta, *The Old Kingdom Art And Archaeology*
M. Bárta (ed.), *The Old Kingdom Art And Archaeology: Proceedings of the Conference held in Prague, May 31-June 4, 2004*, Prague, 2006.

Breasted, *AR* I

J. H. Breasted, *Ancient Records of Egypt*, vol. I. Chicago 1906

Brovarski, *False doors*

E. Brovarski, 'False doors and history; the Sixth Dynasty', *The Old Kingdom Art and Archaeology, Proceedings of the conference held in Prague, May 31-June 4, 2004,* M. Barta (ed.), Prague 2006, pp. 71-118.

Brovarski, *Second Style*

E. Brovarski, 'A Second Style in Egyptian Relief of the Old Kingdom', *Egypt and Beyond, Essays Presented to L.H. Lesko, upon his Retirement from the Wilbour chair of Egyptology at Brown University June 2005,* S.E. Thompson and P. der Manuelian (eds.), Brown University 2008, pp. 69-91.

Brovarski, *Giza Mastabas* 7

E. Brovarski, *The Senedjemib complex*, Part I. *Giza Mastabas*, Vol. 7. Boston 2001.

Cherpion, *Mastabas et hypogées*

N. Cherpion, *Mastabas et hypogées d'Ancien Empire: le problème de la datation*, Bruxelles: 1989.

El-Batal et al., *Gisr el-Mudir I*

A. El-Batal, F. Khattab, S. Soleiman, *The Gisr el-Mudir Cemetery I. The Tombs of Ia-Maat and Others*, Cairo 2012.

Faulkner, *A Concise Dictionary*

R. O. Faulkner, *A Concise Dictionary of Middle Egyptian*, Oxford 1962.

Fischer *Dendera*

H. G. Fischer, *Dendera in The Third Millennium B.C. Down to The Theban Domination of Upper Egypt*, New York, 1986.

Harpur, *Decoration*

Y. Harpur, *Decoration in Egyptian Tombs of the Old Kingdom: Studies in Orientation and Scene Content*, London 1987.

Hassan, *Hemet-Ra*

S. Hassan, *Mastabas of Princess Hemet-Ra and Others. Excavations at Saqqara III (1937-1938)*, Cairo 1975.

Hassan, *Neb-Kaw-Her*
S. Hassan, *The Mastaba of Neb-Kaw-Her. Excavations at Saqqara I (1937-1938)*, Cairo 1975.

Helck, *Untersuchungen*
W. Helck, *Untersuchungen zur Thinitenzeit*, ÄA 45, Wiesbaden 1987.

Houlihan, *Birds*
P. F. Houlihan, *The Birds of Ancient Egypt*, Cairo 1992.

Jones, *Index* I–II
D. Jones, *An Index of the Ancient Egyptian Titles, Epithets and Phrases of the Old Kingdom*, 2 vols., BAR International Series 866, Oxford 2000.

Kanawati, *Administration*
N. Kanawati, *The Egyptian Administration in the Old Kingdom: evidence of its economic decline*, Warminster 1977.

Kanawati, *Conspiracies*
Kanawati, N., *Conspiracies in the Egyptian Palace*, London, New York 2003.

Mathieson et al., *JEA 83*
I. Mathieson, E. Bettles, J. Clarke, C. Duhig, S. Ikram, L. Maguire, S. Quie, A. Tavares, 'The National Museums of Scotland Saqqara Survey Project 1993-1995', *JEA* 83 (1997), pp. 17-33.

Mathieson et al., *JEA 85*
I. Mathieson, E. Bettles, J. Dittmer, C. Reader, 'The National Museums of Scotland Saqqara Survey Project', Earth Sciences 1990-1998, *JEA* 85 (1999), pp. 21-43.

Myśliwiec et.al., *Merefnebef*
K. Myśliwiec et.al., *Saqqara I. The Tomb of Merefnebef*, Warsaw 2004.

Myśliwiec, Kuraszkiewicz et al., *Nyankhnefertem*
K. Myśliwiec, K. Kuraszkiewicz with contributions by A. Kowalska, M. Radomska, T.I. Rzeuska, M. Kaczmarek, I. Kozieradzka, Z. Godziejewski, S. Ikram, A. Zatorska, *Saqqara I. The Funerary Complex of Nyankhnefertem*, Warsaw 2010.

Oxford History
I. Shaw (ed.), *The Oxford History of Ancient Egypt*, Oxford 2000.

Posener-Kriéger, *Archives Neferirkare*
P. Posener-Kriéger, *Les archives du temple funéraire de Néferirkarê-Kakai (Les papyrus d'Abousir) Traduction et commentaire*, vol. I-II, (=BdE 65), Le Caire 1977.

Ranke, *PN*
H. Ranke, *Die ägyptischen Personennamen*, Glückstadt 1935.

Roth, Palace *Attendants*
A.M. Roth, *A Cemetery of Palace Attendants: Including G 2084-2099, G 2230+ 2231, and G 2240,* (=Giza Mastabas 6), Boston 1995.

Russman, Second Style
E. Russman, A Second Style in Egyptian Art of the Old Kingdom, *MDAIK* 51, 1995, 269-279

Simpson, *Giza Mastabas II*
W. K. Simpson, *Giza Mastabas II, The. Mastabas of Qar and Idu*, Boston, 1976.

Strudwick, *The Administration of Egypt*
N. Strudwick, *The Administration of Egypt in the Old Kingdom*, London 1985.

Strudwick, *Texts from the Pyramid Age*
N. C. Strudwick, *Texts from the Pyramid Age*, Atlanta 2005.

Urk. I
K. Sethe, *Urkunden des Alten Reiches*, Leipzig 1933.

Wiebach, *Sheintür*
S. Wiebach, *Die Altägyptische Scheintür. Morphologische Studien zur Entwicklung und Bedeutung der Hauptkultstelle in den Privat-Gräbern des Alten Reiches* (=Hamburger Ägyptologische Studien 1), Hamburg 1981.

INTRODUCTION

In the autumn of year 2008, the Egyptian mission of the Supreme Council of Antiquities (SCA) directed by Zahi Hawass begun a systematic excavation in an area to the south west of the Step Pyramid of Djoser and to the eastern north side from the Pyramid of Unas. The site of the excavation is a part of the area known as Gisr El Mudir, which attracted the scholars' attention since the 90s of the 20th century.[1] In fact, the discovery of the tomb of Qar in 2001 by the Egyptian mission[2] and also the results of the Polish mission[3] endorsed the decision to begin the excavation in the site. The results of the first archaeological season 2008 - 2009 proved that the site hosts a vast cemetery of a middle class officials related to the first half of the 6th Dynasty.[4]

The site chosen for the excavation is located on a hill that was covered with wind-blown sand. On the surface a mixture of *tafla* and limestone could be seen.

---

1 Mathieson et al., *JEA* 83, pp. 17-33; id., *JEA* 85, pp. 21-43.

2 Z. Hawass, *The Tomb of Qar at Saqqara* (in preparation)

3 *Merefnebef*, Myśliwiec et al., *Nyankhnefertem (Saqqara IV)* Mysliwiec, Kuraszkiewicz et al.

4 El-Batal et al., *Gisr el-Mudir I*; Z. Hawass, *The Cemetery of Gisr El Mudir at Saqqara* (in preparation).

CHAPTER ONE

THE TOMB OF IA-MAAT

One of the tombs discovered by the Egyptian mission in 2008 is that of Ia-Maat, which was uncovered during the archaeological season 2009. It is located in the southern west side of the cemetery at a distance of 410 m from the Pyramid of Djoser. It was covered completely with wind blown sand. The tomb was left semi finished; only the lintel on the façade of the cult chapel as well as its south and west walls are decorated with reliefs. The west wall is entirely occupied with a false door sculpted in a plate of fine white limestone. *Fig. 1*

1.1 THE TOMB OWNER AND HIS FAMILY

The name Ia-Maat (*Jꜥ-Mꜣꜥt*) or Ia-Maat-en-Unas (*Jꜥ-Mꜣꜥt-nj-Wnjs*)[5] is the only name of the tomb owner, which is found in the inscriptions of the tomb. This seems to be the first occurrence known of this name. Only one son of the tomb owner, bearing also the name Ia-Maat, is represented and labeled in the tomb; although he is described as *zꜣ.f smsw*, 'his eldest son', no ther names of sons or daughters occur in the inscriptions of the tomb. The tomb owner's wife has not been depicted or mentioned in the tomb. Ia-Maat junior is only depicted on the lintel decorating the façade of the cult chapel.

1.1.1 Titles of the tomb owner

The following titles occur on the façade of the cult chapel on both eastern and western slabs except for the last title which only occurred on the western side of the coffin.

---

5 The name is not recorded by Ranke in *PN*.

jmj-rꜣ jst ḫntj(w)-š pr-ꜥꜣ	assistant overseer of the palace attendants[6].
jmj-rꜣ wpwt Nfr-jswt-Wnjs	overseer of commissions[7] of the pyramid of Unas[8].
jmj-ḫt ḥm(w)-nṯr Nfr-jswt-Wnjs	under-supervisor of *ḥm(w)-nṯr* priests of Unas pyramid[9].
ḥrj-tp ḏꜣt	supervisor of linen[10].
ḫntj-š	attendant[11].
ḫntj-š Nfr-jswt-Wnjs	attendant of Unas pyramid.
ẖrj-ḥꜣbt	lector priest[12].
smr-wꜥtj	sole companion[13].

---

6 Jones, *Index* I, pp. 241, No. 882.

7 Jones, *Index* I, pp. 88-89, No. 375.

8 See also Jones, *Index* I, p. 89, No. 376.

9 Jones, *Index* I. p. 288, No. 1047.

10 This title is only mentioned in the western part of the lintel. For the bibliography of this title see Jones, *Index* II, p. 649, No. 2378.

11 A precise meaning and translation of the title *ḫntj-š* is not yet established. This is due to the fact that the holders of this title were involved in different duties and tasks either during the life of the king or in his funerary complex after his death. For the bibliography and different meanings of the title see Jones, *Index II*, pp. 692-693, No. 2532, especially the interpretation of *ḫntj-š*, as a class of the temple functionaries (Posener-Krieger, *Archives Neferirkare*, pp. 577-581), and as 'guard' (Kanawati, *Conspiracies*, pp. 14-24).

12 Jones, *Index* II, p. 781, No. 2848.

13 Jones, *Index* II, p. 892, No. 3268. The title was among the most frequent titles, especially during the Fourth and the first half of the Fifth Dynasty. During the Sixth Dynasty, the title became only a ranking title. See Helck, *Untersuchungen*, pp. 25, 111; Strudwick, *The Administration of Egypt*, pp. 224-225.

smr pr	companion of the house[14].
sḥḏ ḥm(w)-nṯr nfr-jswt-Wnjs	inspector of *ḥm-nṯr* priests[15] of Unas pyramid.
špsj njswt	noble of the king[16]
ḳbḥ ḥwt-nmt pr-ꜥꜣ	master butcher of the great house[17].

1.1.2 Titles of the son of the tomb owner

jmj-rꜣ jst pr-ꜥꜣ	assistant overseer of the palace.[18]

14 Jones, *Index* II, p. 896, No. 3287.

15 Jones, *Index* II, p. 932, No. 3437.

16 Jones, *Index* II, p. 987, No. 3648.

17 Jones, *Index* II, p. 996, no. 3689.

18 Jones, *Index* II, p.239-40, no. 877.

CHAPTER TWO

TOMB ARCHITECTURE

The rock tomb of Ia-Maat is hewn in the bedrock directly at the eastern wall of an earlier, anonymous large mastaba built of limestone blocks. The arrangement of the two tombs is strikingly similar, e.g., to the tombs of Iyenhor and Hormeru adjoining the mastaba of Nebkauhor.[19] Fig. 2

The tomb consists of two main parts: a) a rectangular east-west cult chapel, cut in the rock and cased with white limestone, entered through a rectangular east west open court; b) the burial shaft.

2.1 THE OPEN COURT

The rectangular court hewn in the bedrock measures 3.20 m (E-W) by 2.30 m (N-S). An L-shaped staircase adjacent to the north and west walls of the court leads from the present surface to the level of the chapel entrance. It consists of 6 small, irregular steps. Four further steps were installed at the western end of these steps. The new steps occupied the lower part of the western wall of the open court. Fig. 3

The walls of the open court were left without smoothing, therefore chisel marks still can be seen on their surface. The floor of the open court is irregular, with a shallow shaft cut into the bedrock of its eastern part. The shaft leads to a small unfinished rectangular burial chamber (2.40 X 1.10 m.). It is evident that the shaft was not in the master plan of the tomb. Its construction caused some damage to the stone blocks of the eastern side of the façade. It seems to be a later addition, executed possibly for a family member who decided to be buried in his/her father's tomb. It is, however, not possible to precisely date the shaft. Fig. 6-8

The south wall of the open court is the façade of the cult chapel.

---

19 Hassan, *Hemet-Ra*, pp. 60, 71; cf. Hassan, *Neb-Kaw-Her*, General plan (no. 22).

2.2 THE CULT CHAPEL

Fig. 8 The entrance to the cult chapel is situated in the middle of its northern wall (south wall of the open court). The height of the facade is 3.9 m, its length 3.20 m. The facade is cased with six courses of yellow limestone blocks that were left rough. The façade is surmounted with a lintel consisting of two long slabs of white limestone, which are decorated with almost symmetrical depictions of the tomb owner and his son.

The western slab measures 1.64 m. in length and 0.38 m. in height, while the eastern slab is 1.56 m. long and 0.38 m high. Above the two slabs the original bedrock is exposed, however, one cannot decide whether this part of the wall was originally covered with limestone or not. The space between the two slabs and the level of the surface of the original bedrock (10.5m high) suggests that it was planned to have it covered; however, the work had never been completed.

The offering chapel is entirely cut into the bedrock and cased with fine limestone slabs on which the figures and the inscriptions were executed.

The entrance to the cult chapel is located in the middle of the façade. It measures 1.62 m. in height, 0.68 m. in width and 0.54 m. in depth.

The chapel is rectangular in plan extending east-west. It measures 2.50 m. in length and 1 m. in width. In the western wall an inscribed false door made of white limestone is embedded, while on the south wall the deceased is depicted in relief, sitting in front of the offering table. A large offering list fills the rest of the surface till the wall's eastern end. Both the eastern and northern walls were left without reliefs. The casing stones of the lower part of the western side of the northern wall are not preserved.

Fig. 17-20 A rectangular slot (0.40 m long, 0.13 m high on the outer side, and 0.40 m long and 0.13m high on the wall's inner side) was cut through the top of the western part of the northern wall. The slot, obviously made for cultic purposes, goes through the entire thickness of the wall. It is aligned with the face of the tomb owner depicted on the southern wall, so that one can see the face through it. Considering that there was no *serdab* or a statue found in the tomb of Ia-Maat, it seems plausible that this hole was used as a kind of *serdab*.

There is a single limestone slab on the chapel's floor, in front of the false door, which was probably supposed to function as an offering table there is no evidence that the whole floor was covered with limestone.

2.3 THE BURIAL SHAFT

Looking for the burial shaft of Ia-Maat's tomb was not by any means an easy task. To the west of the tomb and behind the false door where burial shafts used to be located, there was no space for a shaft, because the area is occupied by the eastern façade of a huge stone mastaba (anonymous mastaba GE001). Also, to the north of the tomb, no space was available, for there is another, relatively small mastaba tomb. Cleaning and excavating the area to the east of Ia-maat's tomb ended up with no results. Also to the south of the tomb we did not expect to find the shaft considering the fact that in this area, attached to the south wall of Ia-Maat's tomb, is an unusual descending entrance leading to the interior of the anonymous tomb GE001, which is located to the west of Ia- Maat. Fig. 33-34

Having checked the area around Ia-Maat's tomb, locating his burial shaft seemed not possible, and doubts about the existence of a burial shaft in this tomb started to rise. It looked as if the tomb had never been used by Ia-Maat.

As the excavation continued in the cemetery, the opening of an isolated burial shaft was found. There was no doubt that the shaft is not related to the tomb of Ia-maat, not only because of its location to the south of the tomb, but also because it constitutes a completely isolated element separated from the chapel of Ia-Maat with the descending entrance to the tomb GE001. To our surprise, the shaft ended with a relatively small burial chamber with a sarcophagus-like burial pit hewn in the rock of the burial-chamber.

The lid of the "sarcophagus" was found in pieces and the archaeological context left no doubts that the burial chamber was disturbed in antiquity. Inside the burial pit a wooden coffin in good condition was found. The names and titles of Ia-Maat are engraved on the outer faces of all the four walls of the coffin and on the top of the lid. Fig. 35-39

Dimensions:

Shaft:	the opening: 1.65 m. X 1.65 m; depth: 5.5 m.
Burial chamber:	length: 2.80 m (north-south); width: 1.40 m (east-west); height: 1 m.
Sarcophagus:	length: 2.20 m (north-south); width: .65 m (east-west); height: 0.65 m.

2.3.1 The inscriptions on the wooden coffin

The lid:

Fig. 35a

ḥtp ḏj njswt Wsjr ḫntj ḏdw ḫp.f ḥr wꜣwt nfr(w)t nt ẖrt-nṯr ḫppt jmꜣḫw ḥr.sn jmj-rꜣ jst ḫntj(w)-š pr-ꜥꜣ Jꜥ-Mꜣꜥt

An offering that the king gives and Osiris, who is in front of Busiris, may he walk on the good roads of the Necropolis on which the revered ones walked, the assistant overseer of the palace attendants, Ia-Maat.

The eastern side:

Fig. 36e

ḥtp ḏj njswt Jnpw ḫntj zḥ-ntr ỉmj-wt nb tꜣ ḏsr prt-ḫrw t ḥnḳt pꜣt n.f m ꜣwt ḏt špsj njswt jmj–rꜣ jst ḫntj(w)-š pr-ꜥꜣ Jꜥ-Mꜣꜥt-n-Wnjs

An offering that the king gives and Anubis, who is in front of the divine shrine, who is in the embalming tent, lord of the Necropolis, invocation offering (consisting of) bread, beer and cake for him in the length of eternity. The noble of the king, overseer of the office of the tenants of the palace, Ia-Maat-en-Unas.

Fig. 36d

The western side:

ḥtp ḏj njswt Wsjr ḫntj ḏdw sm3.f t3 ḏ3.f bj3 m ḥtp m ḥtp ḫr nṯr ˁ3 špsj njswt jmj-r3 jst ḫntj(w)-š pr-ˁ3 Jˁ-M3ˁt-n-Wnjs

An offering that the king gives and Osiris, who is in front of Busiris, may he unite with the earth, may he cross the sky in peace, before the great god, the noble of the king, assistant overseer of the palace attendants, Ia-Maat-en-Unas.[20]

Fig. 35b

The northern side:

jm3ḫw ḫr nṯr ˁ3 Jˁ-M3ˁt-n-Wnjs

The revered one in front of the great god, Ia-Maat-en-Unas.

20 The complete form of Ia-Maat's name appears only on his coffin.

The southern side:

Fig. 35c

jm3ḫw ḳbḥ ḥwt-nmt pr-ʿ3 Jʿ-M3ʿt

The revered one, master butcher of the great house, Ia-Maat

CHAPTER THREE

TOMB DECORATION AND WALL RELIEF PROGRAM

As stated before, the wall relief program of Ia-Maat had never been completed, perhaps due to the sudden death of the tomb owner. The decoration of the two slabs surmounting the façade of the cult chapel, and that of the false door is executed in sunk-relief. Only the depiction of the tomb owner sitting in front of the offering table is executed in bas-relief. A large part of the tomb decoration has not exceeded the first stage of drawing with a black paint or ink.

3.1 THE DECORATION OF THE FAÇADE

On the two slabs decorating the façade, depictions of the tomb owner and his eldest son are sculpted in sunk-relief. There are six figures of the tomb owner and only one depiction of his son on the eastern slab, and five figures of the tomb owner in addition to one figure of his son on the western slab. The figures and the hieroglyphic inscriptions of the eastern slab face the west and read from right to left. On the opposite side, the figures and the hieroglyphic inscriptions read from left to right and face the east. *Fig. 8-9*

3.1.1 The depictions on the eastern slab

One horizontal line of hieroglyphic inscription titles the seven figures, reading from right to left: *Fig. 11-13*

ḥtp dj njswt Jnpw tpj ḏw.f jmj-wt nb tꜣ ḏsr ḳrs.tw.f nfr m js.f n ẖrjt-nṯr m jmꜣḫw ḫr nṯr ꜥꜣ jmj-rꜣ jst ḫntj(w)-š pr-ꜥꜣ Jꜥ-Mꜣꜥt

An offering which the king gives and Anubis, who is on his mountain, who is in the embalming tent, lord of the Necropolis. May he be buried well in his tomb of the cemetery as revered one before the great god, the assistant overseer of the palace attendants, Ia–Maat.[21]

The first depiction of the tomb owner represents him standing facing west, wearing a tight kilt with a belt. He is depicted with a small beard and wearing a long wig that reaches his shoulder. He is holding a long walking stick in his left hand and a scepter in his right hand in a horizontal position. The scepter is depicted as if it goes behind the body of Ia-Maat.

In front of the figure, one column of hieroglyphic inscription reads:

prt ḫrw t ḥnkt pꜣt n špsj njswt smr pr jmꜣḫw Jꜥ-Mꜣꜥt

Invocation offering (consisting of) bread, beer and cake for the noble of the king, companion of the house, revered one, Ia-Maat.

21 For the translation of the title *'jmj-r st ḫntj(w)-š pr ꜥꜣ'* as *'Assistant overseer of the palace attendants'* is following, Roth, *Palace Attendants*, p. 40; Kanawati, *Conspiracies*, pp. 14-24.

The second depiction of Ia-Maat represents him in the same form and attire as the first one. In front of him, one vertical line of inscription reads:

jmj-r3 wpwt Nfr-jswt-Wnjs Jᶜ-M3ᶜt

Overseer of the commissions of Unas pyramid, Ia-Maat.

The third depiction of Ia-Maat represents him in the same form and attire as the previous ones. Only his wig is different; it is a short tight wig with no inner details. He wears no beard. In front of him, one vertical line of inscription reads:

sḥḏ ḥmw-nṯr Nfr-jswt-Wnjs Jᶜ-M3ᶜt

Inspector of ḥmw-nṯr priests of Unas pyramid, Ia-Maat.

The fourth depiction of Ia-Maat represents him in the same form and attire as the first one. In front of him, one vertical line of hieroglyphic inscription reads:

jmj-ḫt ḥmw-nṯr Nfr-jswt-Wnjs Jᶜ-M3ᶜt

Supervisor of the ḥm-nṯr priests of Unas pyramid, Ia-Maat.

The fifth depiction of the tomb owner represents him in the same form and attire as the first depiction. However, a mistake was made by the sculptor with respect to the figure's left hand which is represented as if it were the right one, its details being invisible. In front of Ia-Maat, one vertical line of inscription reads:

ḫntj-š Nfr-jswt-Wnjs Jꜥ-Mꜣꜥt

Attendant of Unas pyramid, Ia-Maat.

The sixth depiction of Ia-Maat represents him in the same form and attire as the third one. The inscription in front of him reads:

smr wꜥtj ẖrj-ḥꜣbt jmꜣḫw Jꜥ-Mꜣꜥt

Sole companion and lector priest, the revered one, Ia-Maat.

The last figure represents the son of the tomb owner wearing a tight kilt with a belt. He is depicted with a small beard and wearing a shoulder-length wig. His left hand is placed on his chest and in the right hand he is holding a bird (Pintail)[22] by the wings as an offering.

In front of this figure, his name, epithets and title are written in a column. The inscription reads:

[22] Houlihan, *Birds*, 71.

zꜣ.f smsw mrj.f jmj-rꜣ jst pr ꜥꜣ Jꜥ-Mꜣꜥt

His eldest son, his beloved, assistant overseer of the palace, Ia–Maat.

3.1.2 THE DEPICTIONS ON THE WESTERN SLAB

Fig. 14-16

All the figures and inscriptions are facing left, i.e. eastwards.

One horizontal line of hieroglyphic inscription titles the six figures reading from left to right:

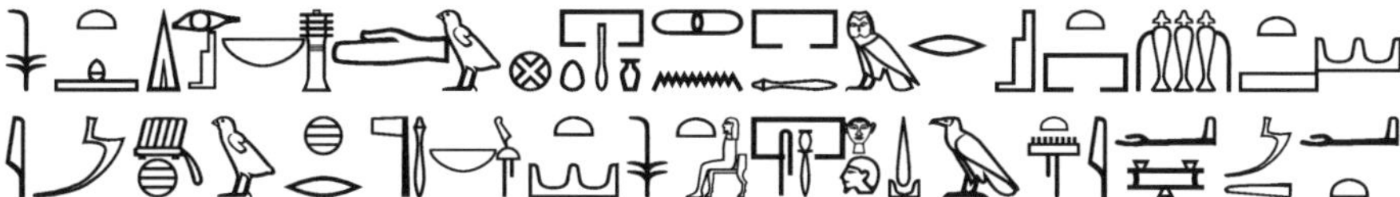

ḥtp ḏj njswt Wsjr nb ḏdw prt ḫrw t ḥnkt pꜣt n jmj-rꜣ jst ḫntj(w)-š pr ꜥꜣ jmꜣḫw ḫr nṯr ꜥꜣ nb jmnt špsj njswt smr pr ḥrj-tp ḏꜣt Jꜥ-Mꜣꜥt

An offering which the king gives and Osiris, lord of Djedu. Invocation offering (consisting of) bread, beer and cake to the assistant overseer of the palace attendants, revered one before the great god, lord of the west, noble of the king, companion of the house, supervisor of linen Ia-Maat.

The first figure is a depiction of the tomb owner standing, wearing a tight kilt with a belt. He is depicted with a small beard and wearing a shoulder-length wig. He is holding a long walking stick with his left hand and a scepter in his right hand. Like in the fifth figure on the estern slab, the sculptor failed to show the right positions of the two hands of the tomb owner, as a result the two hands appeared as two left hands.

In front of the figure, one vertical line of inscription is written. It reads:

prt-ḫrw t ḥnḳt pꜣt n špsj njswt smr pr jmꜣḫw Jꜥ-Mꜣꜥt

Invocation offering (consisting of) bread, beer and cake to the noble of the king, companion of the house, the revered one Ia-Maat.

The second depiction of Ia-Maat represents him in the same form and attire as the previous one. Only his wig is different; it is a short tight wig with no inner details. He wears no beard. The inscription in front of him reads:

jmj-rꜣ wpwt Nfr-jswt-Wnjs Jꜥ-Mꜣꜥt

Overseer of the commissions of Unas pyramid Ia-Maat.

The third figure represents Ia-Maat in the same attire as the first one. However, the bottom line of the front pleated part of the kilt is shown in this case. The inscription in front of him reads:

sḥḏ[23] *ḥm(w) nṯr Nfr-jswt-Wnjs Jꜥ-Mꜣꜥt*

Inspector of the priests of Unas pyramid Ia-Maat.

---

23 The artist misplaced the sign s.

The fourth figure represents Ia-Maat in the same form and attire as the second one, with more details added: a wide collar around his neck and a bracelet on his right hand's wrist. Also, the walking stick is now depicted in the right hand of Ia-Maat, and the scepter in his left hand. The inscription in front of him reads:

jmj-ḫt ḥm(w)-nṯr Nfr-jswt-Wnjs Jˁ–M3ˁt

Supervisor of the ḥm(w)-nṯr priests of Unas pyramid Ia-Maat.

The fifth figure is depicted more completely than all other ones. The tomb owner, wearing a shoulder-length wig with details of the hair and traces of black color, a tight kilt, a wide collar around his neck and bracelets on his right and left hand wrists. He is holding a long walking stick in his right hand and a scepter in his left hand. Traces of red color can still be seen on his body. The inscription in front of him reads:

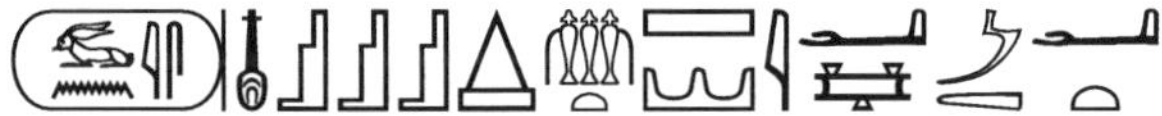

ḫntj-š Nfr-jswt-Wnjs Jˁ–M3ˁt

Attendant of Unas pyramid Ia-Maat.

The last figure represents the son of the tomb owner, wearing a tight kilt with a belt and a short tight wig. Retouches were made by the sculptor in the area of the head. The son is depicted holding two birds in each hand by the wings (Pintail). The inscription in front of him reads:

zꜣ.f smsw mrj.f jmj-rꜣ jst pr ꜥꜣ Jꜥ–Mꜣꜥt

His eldest son, his beloved, assistant overseer of the palace, Ia–Maat.

3.2 INTERIOR OF THE CHAPEL: DECORATION OF THE SOUTH INNER WALL

Fig. 20-32 The relief program of the small cult chapel has never been completed. Only one scene is depicted on the south wall of the cult chapel in its western part. It represents the tomb owner sitting at an offering table, and an almost complete offering list that spans the upper part of the southern wall.

3.2.1 The offering scene

A large figure of the tomb owner sitting on a low back seat is the only motif represented on the south wall. Ia-Maat is depicted in bas-relief on the western side of the wall, sitting on a low back seat with animal shaped *Fig. 25-26* legs. He is facing east, wearing a tight kilt and a shoulder-length wig. Details of the wig are rendered with precision and skill. A wide collar is depicted around his neck. Th e tomb owner is holding a handkerchief in his left hand, while reaching the offering table with his stretched right hand. Above the offering table loaves of bread represented as a *sht* field are depicted in an upright position, being divided into two symmetrical parts. Under and beside the table heaps of fruit, vegetables and cuts of meat are depicted. Also, a large jar is depicted placed on a stand.

Above the depiction of Ia-maat, three horizontal lines of inscription are written with black paint. The inscription reads from east to west:

Fig. 27

ḥtp dj njswt Jnpw tpj ḏw.f n jm3ḫw Jꜥ-M3ꜥt
prt-ḫrw t ḥnḳt p3t n špsj njswt smr pr Jꜥ–M3ꜥt
jmj-r3 jst ḫntj(w)-š pr-ꜥ3 Jꜥ-M3ꜥt

An offering which the king gives and Anubis, who is on his mountain, to the revered one, Ia-Maat
Invocation offerings (consisting of) bread, beer and cake for the noble of the king, companion of the house, Ia-Maat.
Assistant overseer of the palace attendants, Ia-Maat.

Behind the tomb owner's figure, the seven sacred oils are depicted in five sub-registers. The first four oils are represented in the upper two registers, while the other three in the lower three subsidiary registers, each one in one of them. The depiction of the seven sacred oils in subsidiary registers behind the scene of the tomb owner sitting at the offering table is unique in the newly discovered cemetery of Gisr El Mudir. Two different types of vessels are depicted as containers of the sacred oils, namely a jar and a cup.

In the first upper subsidiary register, a jar and a cup are depicted in bas-relief from left to right (east to west), however, traces of black paint still can be seen on them. Above each container the name of the sacred oil is written with black paint. The sculptor was about to start cutting the relief when his work was stopped. The two names read from left to right:

sṯ-ḥ3b, ḥknw

In the second subsidiary register a cup and a jar are depicted in bas-relief with traces of black paint. Above each depiction the name of the oil is written in sunk-relief. The two names read:

sfṯ, nẖnm.

The third subsidiary register shows one oil cup depicted with black paint. The name of the oil is also written with black paint above the cup:

tw3wt.

The fourth subsidiary register only shows only one jar depicted in black paint, with the name of the oil written equally with black paint above the cup. The hieroglyphic signs are in a bad state of preservation, and cannot be read. However, it is easy to recognize the name of the missing oil in the list, which is *ḥ3tt ʿš* (best cedar oil).

The bottom subsidiary register shows a container of sacred oil depicted with black paint. The name of the oil is written with black paint in front of the cup. It name reads:

ḥ3tt ṯḥnw (best Libyan oil).

In front of the tomb owner's face and chest, a list of the six main offerings is depicted into two vertical sections that read from up down, right to left (west to east):

ẖ3 t ẖ3 ḥnkt ẖ3 k3w ẖ3 3bd ẖ3 šsr ẖ3 mnẖt

Thousand of bread, thousand of beer, thousand of cows, thousand of birds, thousand of vessels, thousand of linen.

3.2.2 The offering list

Above the offering table, a large extended offering list is depicted into two horizontal sections. Each offering commodity and ritual is depicted in one single column followed by the number or the amount of the commodity that the tomb owner desires to have. The lower section of the list was mostly cut in sunk-relief, while the upper part of the list is depicted in black paint. 92 offerings and rituals are written in the list from right to left (west to east):

1- *Mw sṯw*– water for libation, one Fig. 28
2- *snṯr sḏt*– lighted incense
3- *sṯ–ḥb* -oil
4- *ḥknw* -oil
5- *sfṯ* -oil
6- *nẖnm* -oil
7- *tw3wt* -oil
8- *ḥ3tt ʿš* -best cedar oil
9- *ḥ3tt ṯḥnw* -best Libyan oil
10- *w3ḏ ʿrf* -bag of green paint, two
11- *msdt ʿrf* -bag of black paint, two
12- *wnẖ* -cloth strips
13- *snṯr sḏt* -lighted incense
14- *ḳbḥw ṯ3wy*- libation water and, two balls
15- *ẖ3t* -offering table, one
16- *ḥtp njswt* -royal offering, one
17- *ḥtp njswt jmj wsẖt* -royal offering which is in the *wsẖt*-hall, two
18- *ḥms* – sit down, once
19- *šns n jʿw-r3* – bread of breakfast, two Fig. 29
20- *t-wt* –bread, one
21- *t rtḥ* – bread
22- *nmst ḥnḳt* – jug of beer, one
23- *šns ʿnf* – bread, one
24- *šns šbw* – bread of main meal
25- *swt* – piece of meat, one

26- *ʿ mw* – bowl of water, two
27- *db ʿ* – bowl of natron, two
28- *šns jʿw r šns* – bread of breakfast
30- *t rtḥ* – *rtḥ*-bread, one
31- *ḥṯw* – *ḥṯw*-bread, two
32- *nḥrw* – *nḥrw*-bread, two
33- *dpꜣ* – *dpꜣ*-bread, four
34- *psʿ* – *psʿ*-bread, four
35- *šns* – *šns*-bread, four
Fig. 30 36- *t jmj-tꜣ* – *jmj-tꜣ*-bread, four
37- *ẖnfw ʿ* – bowl of *ẖnfw*-bread, four
38- *ḥbnnw*t *ʿ* – bowl of *ḥbnnwt*-bread, four
39- *jdꜣt-ḥꜣk* – *jdꜣt-ḥꜣk* -bread, four
40- *pꜣwt* – *pꜣwt*–bread, four
41- *t ꜣšrt* – *ꜣsrt*-bread, four
42- *ḥḏw ʿ* – bowl of onions, four
43- *ẖpš* – foreleg, one
44- *jwʿ* – thigh, one
45- *sẖn* – kidney, one
46- *swt* – piece of meat, one
47- *spḥt* – rib, one
48- *mjst* – liver, one
49- *nnšm* – spleen, one
50- *ḥʿ* – piece of meat, one
Fig. 28 51- *jwf ḥꜣt* – fillet, one
52- *srw*– *srw*-goose, one
53- *ṯrp*– *ṯrp*-goose, one
54- *st* – duck, one
55- *sr* – *sr*-goose, one
56- *mnwt* – pigeon, one
57- *t sjf* – *sjf*-bread, one
58- *šʿt* – *šʿt*-bread, two
59- *npꜣwt ʿ* – bowl of *npꜣwt*-bread, two
60- *mswt ʿ* – bowl of *mswt*-bread, two
61- *ḏsrt ʿ* – bowl of *ḏsrt*-beverage, two

62- *ḏsrt j3tt* – bowl of milky beverage, two
63- *ḥnḳt ḫnms* – bowl of *ḫnms*-beer, two
64- *ḥnḳt* ʿ – bowl of beer
65- *sḫpt* ʿ – bowl of *sḫpt* – beverage, two
66- *pḫ3* ʿ – bowl of *pḫ3* beverage, two
67- *ḏwjw sšr* – jug of *sšr*-beverage, two
68- *d3b* ʿ – bowl of figs, two
69- *jrp* ʿ – bowl of wine, two *Fig. 29*
70- *ʿbš jrp jmtj* – bowl of *ʿbš-jmtj* wine, two
71- *jrp snwt* – bowl of *snwt*-wine, two
72- *jrp ḥ3mw* – bowl of *ḥ3mw*-wine, two
73- *ḥbnnwt* ʿ – bowl of *ḥbnnwt*-bread, two
74- *ḫnfw* ʿ – bowl of *ḫnfw*-bread, two
75- *jšd* ʿ – bowl of *išd*-fruit, two
76- *sḫt ḥḏt* ʿ – bowl of *sḫt ḥḏt*-fruit, two
77- *sḫt w3ḏt* ʿ – bowl of *sḫt ḥḏt*-fruit, two
78- *ʿwgt swt* ʿ – bowl of special preparation of wheat
79- *ʿwgt jt* ʿ – bowl of special preparation of barley
80- *b3b3t* ʿ – bowl of *b3b3t* fruit, two
81- *nbs* ʿ – bowl of *nbs*-fruit, two
82- *t nbs* ʿ – bowl of *nbs*-bread, two
83- *wʿḥ* ʿ – bowl of carob beans, two
84- *ḫt nbt bnrt* – every sweet thing, two
85- *rnpt* – the year-offering, one
86- *ḥnkt* – *ḥnkt*-offering, one *Fig. 30*
87- *gsw* – half-loaves, one
88- *stp ḫpš* – the choice foreleg, one
89- *ḥʿt wdḥw* – best offerings, one
90- *wḏb* – provisions, one
91- *sṯw* – purification water, one
92- *snṯr* – incense, one
93- *jnt rd* – rite of bringing the foot.[24]

[24] This ritual started to appear as early as the Fifth dynasty see Barta, *Opferliste*, pp. 71-2 and 86.

3.3 THE FALSE DOOR (WEST WALL)

The west wall of the cult chapel of Ia-Maat is entirely occupied by one monolithic false door made of white limestone, which is 1.55 m high and 1.00 m wide.

The false door consists of a relatively narrow recessed panel which constitutes the actual doorway topped with a semi-cylindrical molding representing the reed mat generally used to close a real door. The recessed panel and the molding are set inside a rectangular frame consisting of two door-jambs and a lintel, topped by a rectangular panel depicting the tomb owner sitting on a low back chair with lion-shaped legs in front of an offering table loaded with bread. The tomb owner is facing right (north), and reaching the bread with his left hand. Above him an abbreviated offering formula is inscribed. An architrave and two jambs frame the rectangular panel. All components were set inside an outer frame. The inscriptions on each of the three sets of jambs are almost identical, and each vertical line ends with a standing figure of the tomb owner holding a walking stick and a scepter in his hands. The false door is placed on a stone platform, its shape conforms to the later Old Kingdom false doors form with the cavetto cornice and torus molding which, developed from the beginning of the Fifth dynasty to the end of the Sixth dynasty.[25]

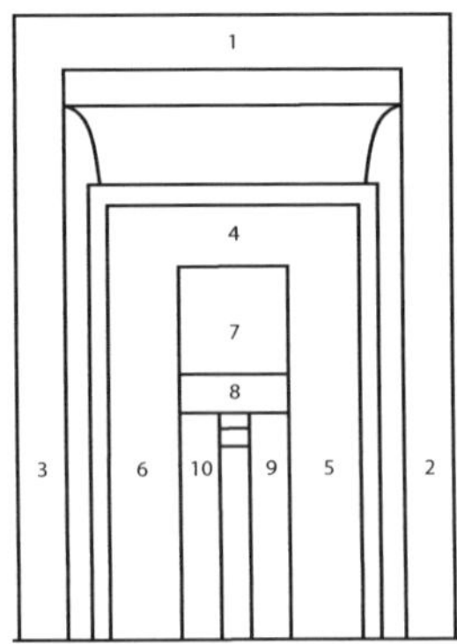

[25] Strudwick, *Administration*, p. 9ff.; Wiebach, *Scheintür*, pp. 133-35,

The inscriptions on the false door are:

1.

prt-ḫrw t ḥnḳt pꜣt n špsj njswt smr pr jmj-rꜣ jst ḫntj(w)-š pr-ꜥꜣ Jꜥ-Mꜣꜥt

Invocation offering (consisting of) bread, beer and cake for the noble of the king, companion of the house, assistant overseer of the palace attendants, Ia-Maat.

2. 

ḥtp ḏj njswt Wsjr nb ḏdw n jmꜣḫw ḫr nṯr-ꜥꜣ nb jmnt Jꜥ-Mꜣꜥt

An offering which the king gives (and) Osiris, lord of Busiris, to the revered one before the great god, lord of the west,[26] *Ia-Maat.*

3. 

ḥtp ḏj njswt Jnpw tpj ḏw.f jmj-wt nb tꜣ ḏsr ḳrs.tw.f nfr jmꜣḫw Jꜥ–Mꜣꜥt

An offering which the king gives (and) Anubis, who is upon his mountain, who is in the embalming tent, lord of the Necropolis, that he may be buried well, the revered one, Ia–Maat.

4.

prt-ḫrw t ḥnkt pꜣt n smr wꜥtj ẖrj–ḥꜣbt Jꜥ-Mꜣꜥt

Invocation offering (consisting of) bread, beer and cake to the sole companion, the lector priest, Ia-Maat.

[26] Jones, *Index* I, p. 31, No. 145.

5.

špsj njswt smr pr jmj-rꜣ jst ẖntj(w)-š pr-ꜥꜣ Jꜥ-Mꜣꜥt

Noble of the king, the companion of the house, assistant overseer of the palace attendants, Ia-Maat.

6.

špsj njswt smr pr jmj-rꜣ jst ẖntj(w)-š pr-ꜥꜣ Jꜥ-Mꜣꜥt

Noble of the king, the companion of the house, assistant overseer of the palace attendants, Ia-Maat.

7.

ḥtp ḏj njswt n jmꜣẖw Jꜥ-Mꜣꜥt

An offering which the king gives to the revered one, Ia-Maat.

8.

jmꜣẖw Jꜥ-Mꜣꜥt

Revered one, Ia–Maat.

9 and 10

prt-ẖrw t ḥnkt pꜣt n jmꜣẖw Jꜥ-Mꜣꜥt

Invocation offering (consisting of) bread, beer and cake for the revered one, Ia-Maat.

CHAPTER FOUR

DATING THE TOMB OF IA-MAAT

Dating an ancient Egyptian tomb is indeed the most arduous of all research projects in the field of Egyptology. The difficulty of the process of identifying the exact date of a tomb lies in the rarity of the inclusion of dates in the tomb's decorative scheme. Also, the nature of the dating system devised by the ancient Egyptians adds another layer of difficulty. In such system, the event of a king's ascension to the throne of Egypt is considered *the* defining moment in history to which *all* dated events are linked in a time referential. In other words, the events that occurred during the reign of a certain king were linked in time with the moment of his ascension and identified by year, day, month and season of the reigning king. The system of referentiality to multiple defining moments (i.e. kings' ascensions to the throne) resulted in the absence of continuous dates for historical events and individuals' achievements.[27]

Striving to identify criteria for dating tombs and documents, Egyptologists have adopted different approaches to the pictorial and textual records in hand. Principal among these records are the Old Kingdom biographical inscriptions on tomb walls.[28] They traditionally contain references to kings, and could be analyzed in order to establish the date of the tomb. However, it is always advised against a heavy reliance on the mere mention of a king's name in the tomb inscriptions, particularly in the case of priests or administrators employed at royal funerary establishments. The King's name in such case is misleading as these funerary establishments were functioning even after the death of their kings, and younger generations of administrators and priests were employed in order to maintain the cult of these already dead kings.

27 Shaw, *Oxford History*, pp. 1-15

28 Breasted, *AR*, vol. I; Strudwick, *Texts from The Pyramid Age*.

In this regard, Klaus Baer[29] and Naguib Kanawati[30] have made significant strides in reconstructing the skeleton of Egypt's administrative system, depending in most part on the administrative titles recorded on the different architectural elements of the tomb and integrated in the "auto-biographical" texts. Their monumental works were supplemented by N. Strudwick's careful analysis of the same records, in addition to tracing the evolvement of the false door in these tombs, not only as an architectural element, but also as a medium of transcription for administrative titles.[31] Moreover, the importance of the false door as an architectural element that carries dating criteria was further underlined by E. Brovarski. He analyzed the scene of the deceased and the offering table that customarily appears on the panel or tablet of the false door.[32] He identified several components of that scene that are indicators of certain periods. N. Cherpion also focused on the development of certain scenes and attire.[33]

Adopting the same apparatus of scene analysis, Y. Harpur carefully studied the decorative program of wall relief in the Old Kingdom mastabas.[34] She paid considerable attention to the distribution of scenes on the walls of the different chambers and galleries of the mastabas, and highlighted a number of dating criteria as to the development of the decorative program of the wall relief. The thoroughness of her study made it indeed invaluable to the process of dating Old Kingdom tombs. In addition, scenes of the private tombs were subject to art analysis by E. Russman and E. Brovarski.[35] They theorize that the end of the Old Kingdom, particularly from the reign of King Pepy I on, is marked by major stylistic changes in the execution of human figures, both in two dimensional and three dimensional sculptures. Russman identified characteristics of the late

29 Baer, *Rank and Title.*

30 Kanawati, *Administration.*

31 Strudwick, *The Administration of Egypt.*

32 E. Brovarski, *False doors*, pp. 71-118.

33 Cherpion, *Mastabas et hypogées.*

34 Harpur, *Decoration.*

35 E. Brovarski, *Second Style*, pp. 69-91.

Dynasty Six reliefs, referring to the artistic style of that period as the "Second Style of Art" of the Old Kingdom.[36] In a lengthy article, Brovarski expounded on Russman's analysis, and identified more characteristics of the "Second Style of Art".

Moreover, H. Fischer relied on the paleographical evolution of the hieroglyphic signs as well as the orthographical changes of proper names commonly used in formulae in order to date the corpus of the First Intermediate Period epigraphical materials from Dendara.[37] Fischer, later joined by Brovarski, focused the paleographical and orthographical analyses on the offering formula.

The tomb of Ia-maat lies in a very close proximity to the Pyramid of King Unas in the Cemetery known as Gisr Al-Mudir. This cemetery includes several types of tombs. Some tombs are built on the traditional mastaba form without courts or interior chapels, while others are designed with a court sunken into the ground. Such court is accessible through rock-cut steps. The latter type of mastabas has rock-cut chapels as well, and burial shafts behind the false door.

This cemetery seems that have been founded in the early years of Dynasty Six. Inscriptions in many of the Gisr Al-Mudir tombs were subject to alterations. So far, we know about one case in which a tomb was reassigned to a female singer after it was taken away from its original owner. The offering formula and the titles of the new tomb owner were applied on a thin layer of red plaster right on top of the old inscription that was cut into the rock. Also, evidence of *Damnatio memoriae* is found in that cemetery. In a recently discovered tomb, the name of King Unas has faced acts of erasure, where it was partially removed from the architrave inscription. Ironically, the inscription mentions that Unas commissioned the cutting of a sarcophagus of Tura fine white limestone as well as its transportation to the tomb on a large barge.

Indeed, these acts of reassignment of tombs and alteration of tomb inscriptions have been already met with in the cemetery of the "royal guards" located around the causeway of Unas's pyramid. Kanwati

36 E. Russmann, *Second Style*, pp. 269-79.

37 Fischer, *Dendera*.

postulates that the reassignment of the tombs of the "royal guards" is an indication of their evolvement in a conspiracy against the King.[38] This calls to attention the political unrest at the early years of the Sixth Dynasty. From that period, indications are that King Userkare, the second King of the Sixth Dynasty, has assassinated his predecessor. We also learn from the autobiography of Weni of what could be a Harem conspiracy in the court of King Pepy I.[39]

In this regard, it should be noted that the full name of Ia-maat includes the element Unas, reading Ia-maat-n-Unas. It is only found on the wooden coffin, and appears nowhere else in the tomb. In fact, the concealment of the name of Unas in the tomb of Ia-maat is another incident of deliberate attack on the memory of King Unas. Chronologically speaking, the concealment of Unas's name signals to the early years of Dynasty Six as a possible date for the tomb of Ia-maat.

Like the tomb of Qar at Giza,[40] the architectural layout of Ia-maat's tomb conforms to the type of tombs that consist of a rock-cut chapel and a forecourt reachable through rock-cut steps. Such design is very well known from the time of King Pepy I and continued to the end of Dynasty Six.

Although, the tomb of Ia-maat is not fully decorated, its wall reliefs conform to the canonical program of tomb decoration set at the time of King Pepy I and continued well into the time of Pepy II. Significant among the elements of such program is the multiple representation of the deceased standing in full regalia holding a scepter. Such scene traditionally occupies the architrave of the chapel. In the tomb of Ia-maat, we see that scene decorating the architrave of Ia-maat's chapel.

Stylistically, characteristics of the "Second Style of Old Kingdom Art", which appeared at the end of the reign of King Pepy I, are present in the figures of Ia-maat represented on the architrave. Ia-maat's figures show slender and long arms, without muscle rendition. Legs lack muscle

---

38 Kanawati, *Conspiracies.*

39 *Urk. I*, pp. 98-109.

40 Simpson, *Giza Mastabas II.*

rendition as well. Shoulders are wide and waist is narrow. However, several other characteristics of the "Second Style of Art" are absent, like the pushed up waist and disproportionate head on a wide shoulder. Figures of Ia-maat might have been executed according to artistic tradition that preceded the prevalence of the "Second Style of Art".

On the long wall of the chapel, a long offering list, categorically known as Type A List by Barta,[41] is inscribed. It is however unfinished. Such tyw toward the end of Dynasty Six. This means that the tomb of Ia-maat should be placed right in the end of King Pepy I's reign and the early years of King Pepy II. This date could be corroborated by the type of false door of Ia-maat.

---

41 Barta, *Opferliste*.

LIST OF FIGURES

27. *Southern wall of the chapel – fragment a.*
28. *Southern wall of the chapel – offering list, fragment b.*
29. *Southern wall of the chapel – offering list, fragment c.*
30. *Southern wall of the chapel – offering list, fragment d.*
31. *Southern wall of the chapel – representation of Ia-Maat at the offering table.*
32. *Detail of the above.*
33. *The burial shaft seen from above.*
34. *Embedded sarcophagus in the burial chamber.*

35-36 *Coffin of Ia-Maat – a) lid; b) northern side; c) southern side; d) western side; e) eastern side.*

37. *The wooden coffin of Ia-Maat.*

38-39. *Coffin: details of the eastern side.*

FIGURES

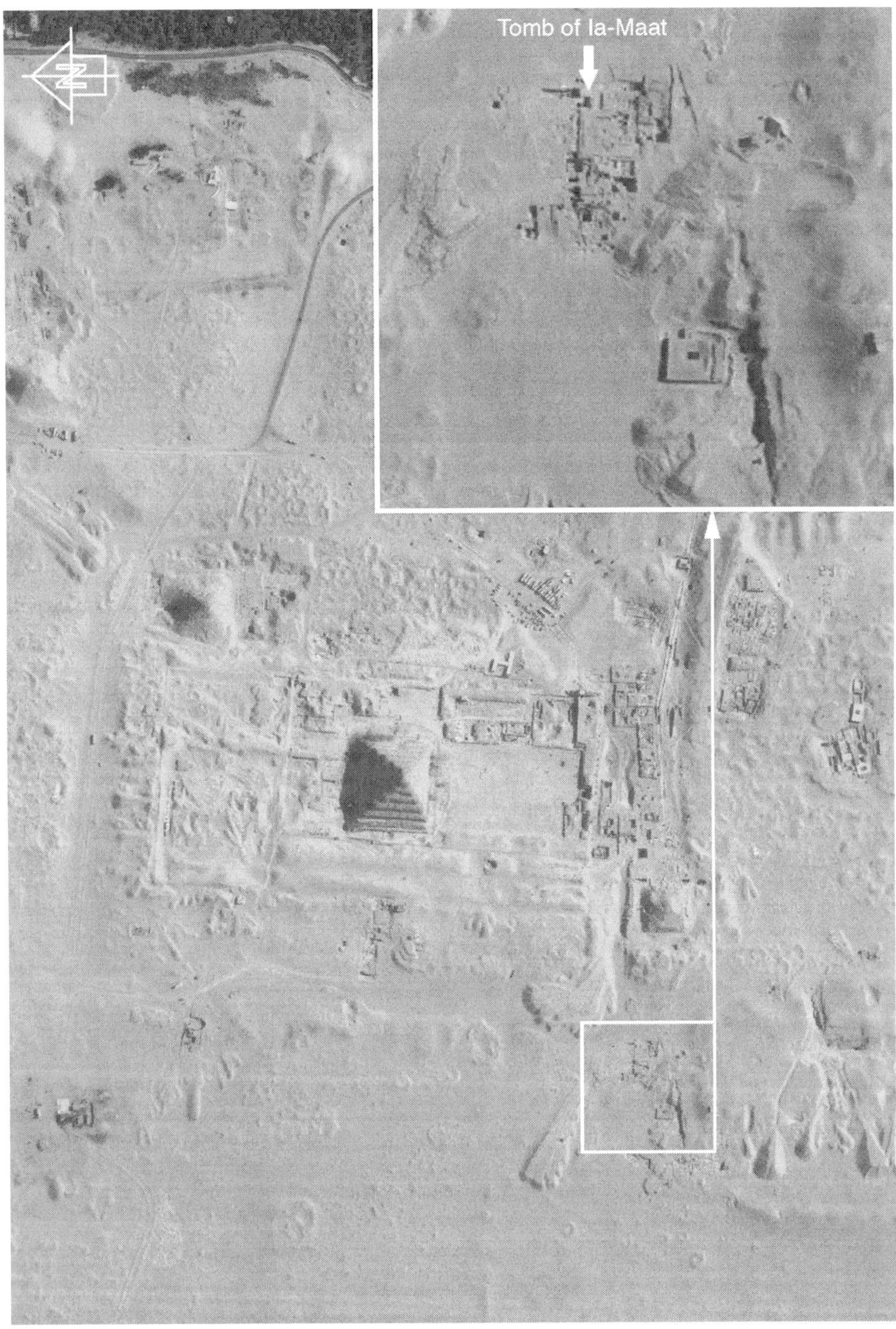

Fig. 1. Position of the tomb of Ia-Maat.

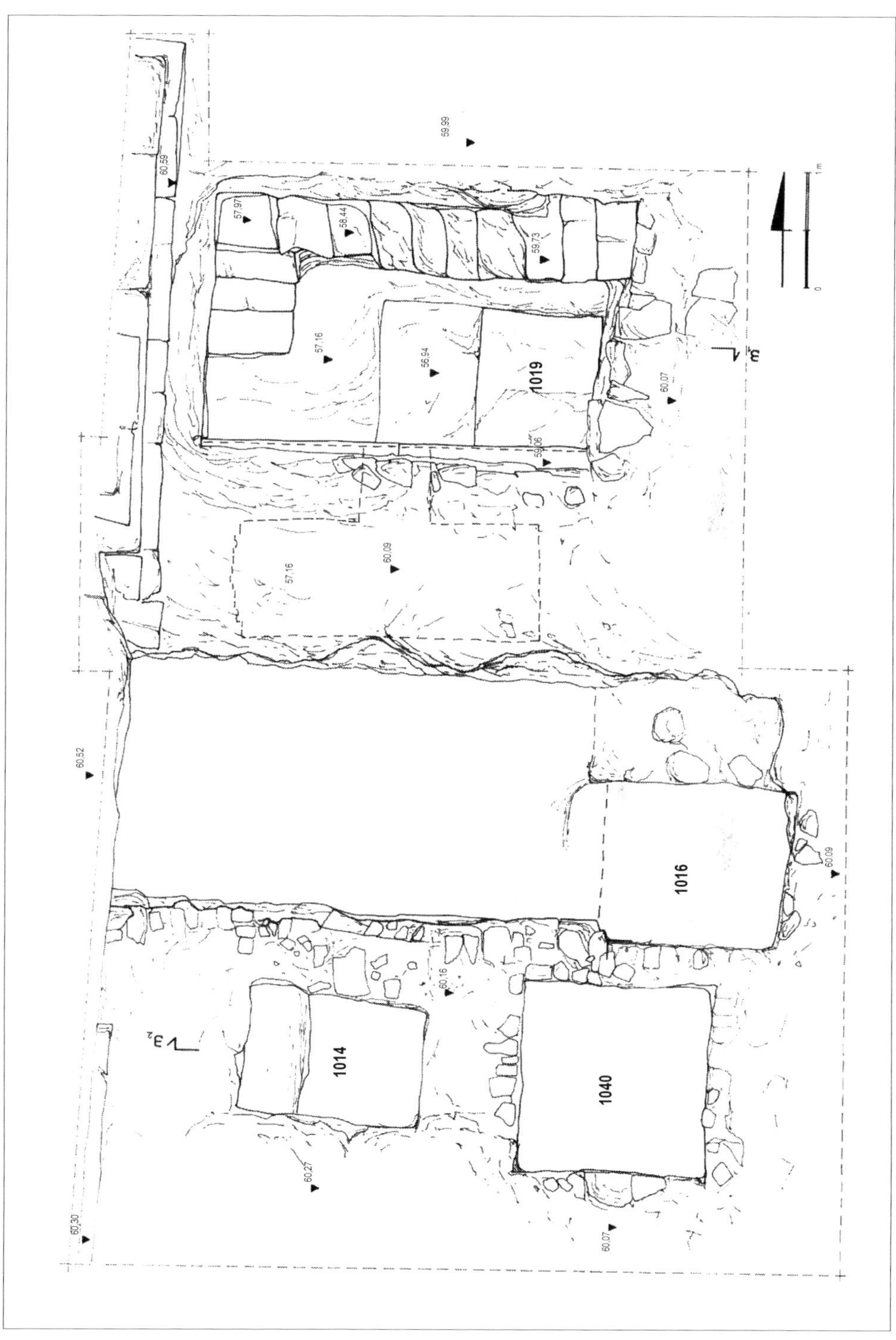

Fig. 2. General plan.

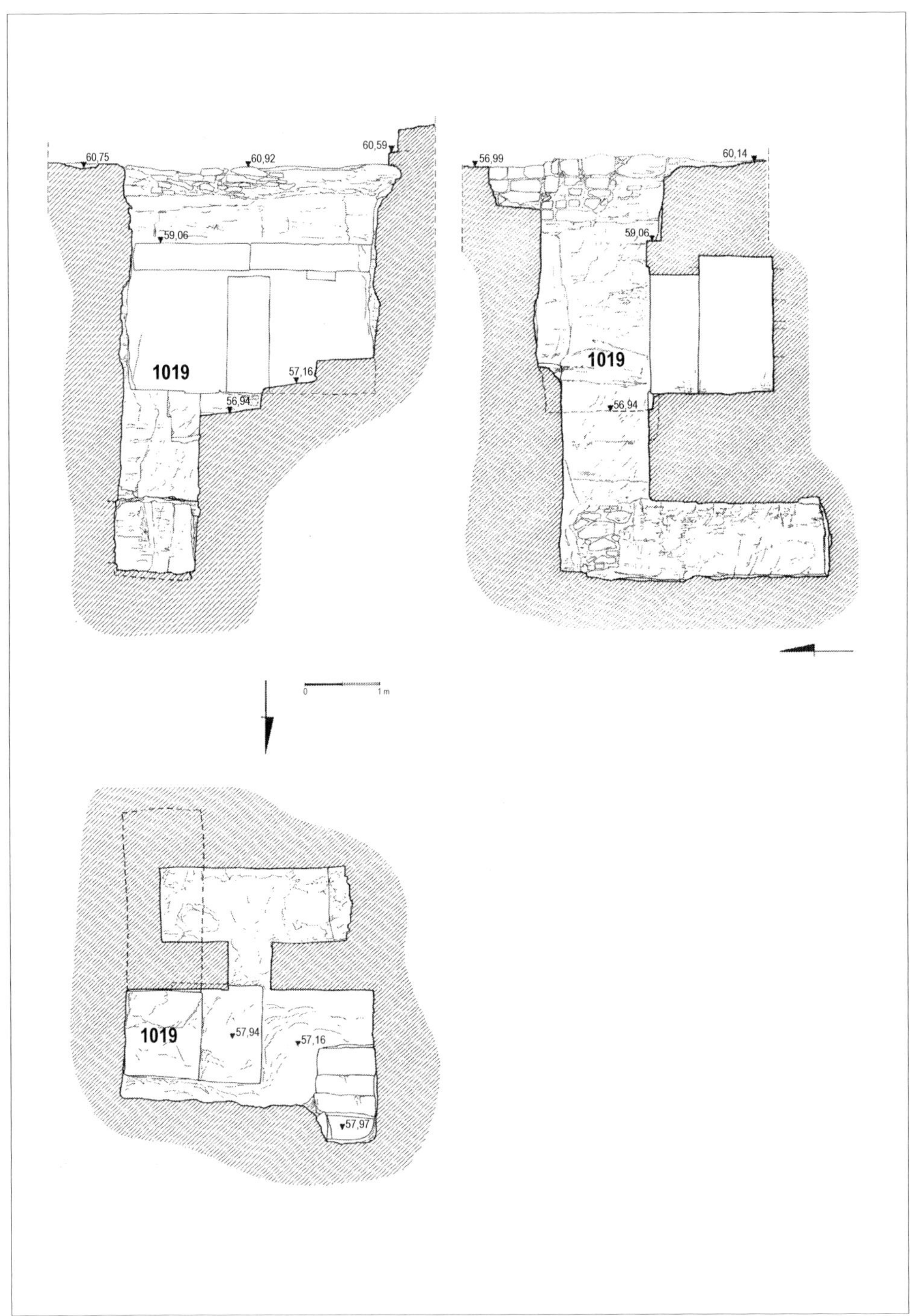

Fig. 3. Cross-sections and plan of the chapel and shaft 1019.

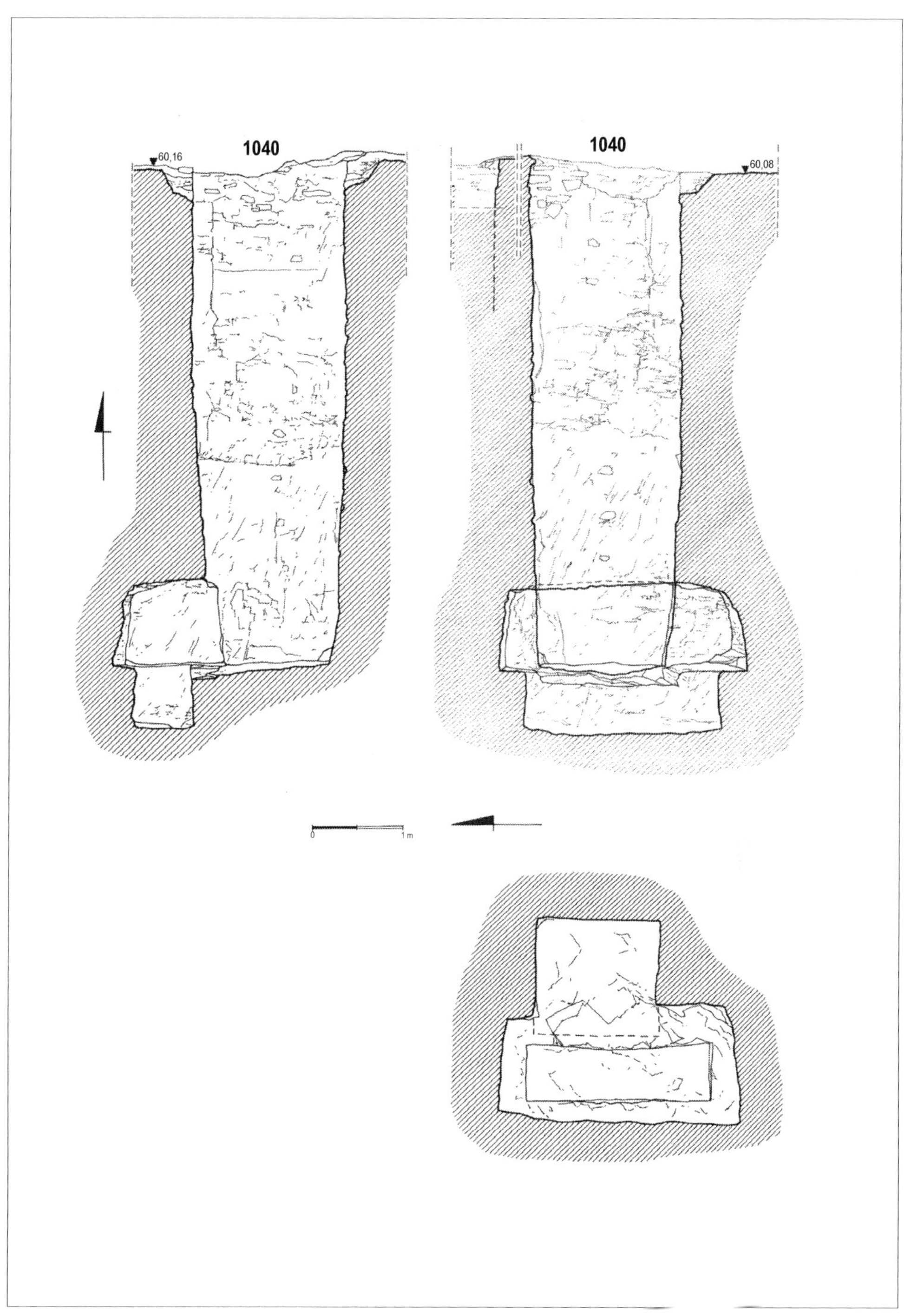

Fig. 4. Cross-sections of shaft 1040 and plan of the burial chamber.

Fig. 5. General view of the excavation site.

Fig. 6. Tomb of Ia-Maat; view from the west.

Fig. 7. Open court; view from the south.

Fig. 8. Open court, view from the north.

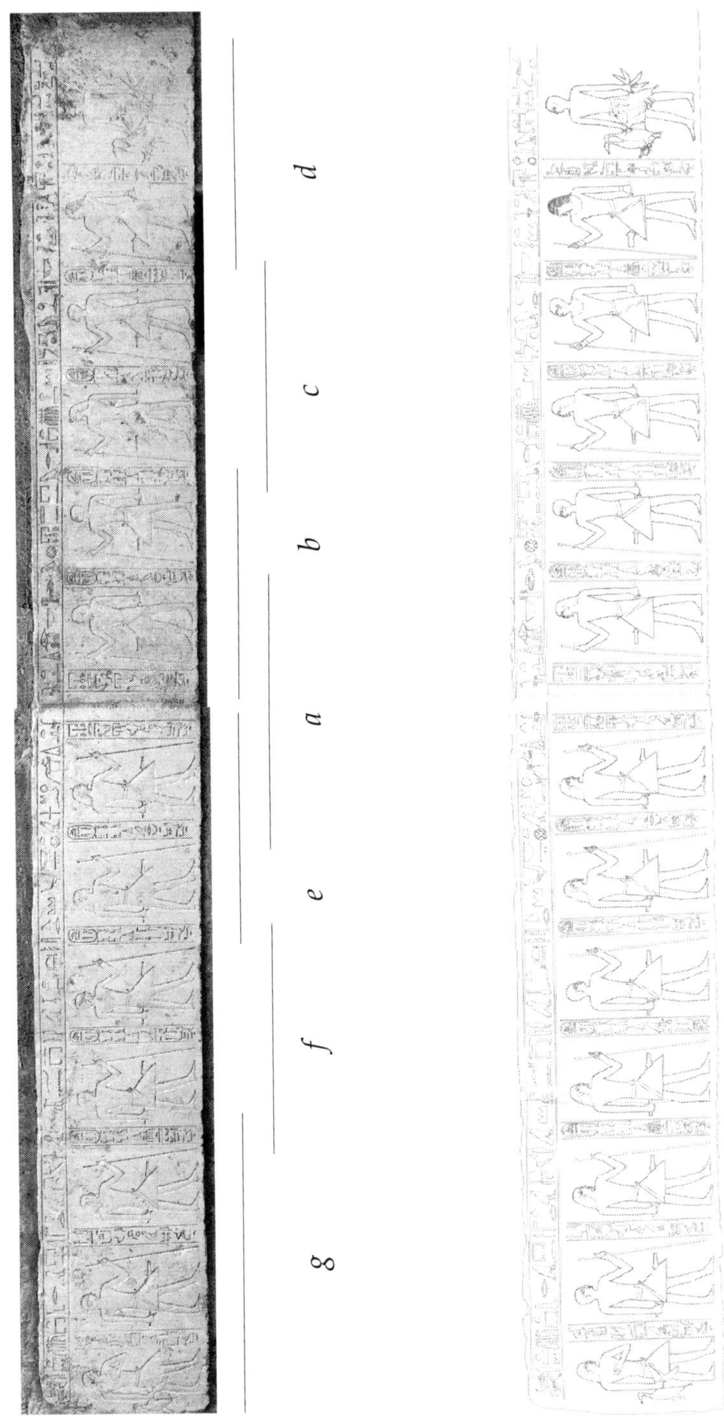

Fig. 9. Lintel above the entrance to the chapel.

Fig. 10. Lintel above the entrance to the chapel – fragment a.

Fig. 14. Lintel above the entrance to the chapel – fragment b.

Fig. 15. Lintel above the entrance to the chapel – fragment c.

Fig. 16. Lintel above the entrance to the chapel – fragment d.

Fig. 11. Lintel above the entrance to the chapel – fragment e.

Fig. 12. Lintel above the entrance to the chapel – fragment f.

Fig. 13. Lintel above the entrance to the chapel – fragment g.

Fig. 17. Facade of the chapel with the rectangular slot under the lintel.

Fig. 18. The rectangular slot in the western part of the facade.

Fig. 19. View into the chapel through the rectangular slot.

Fig. 20. The rectangular slot in the facade – view from the chapel.

Fig. 21-22. False door.

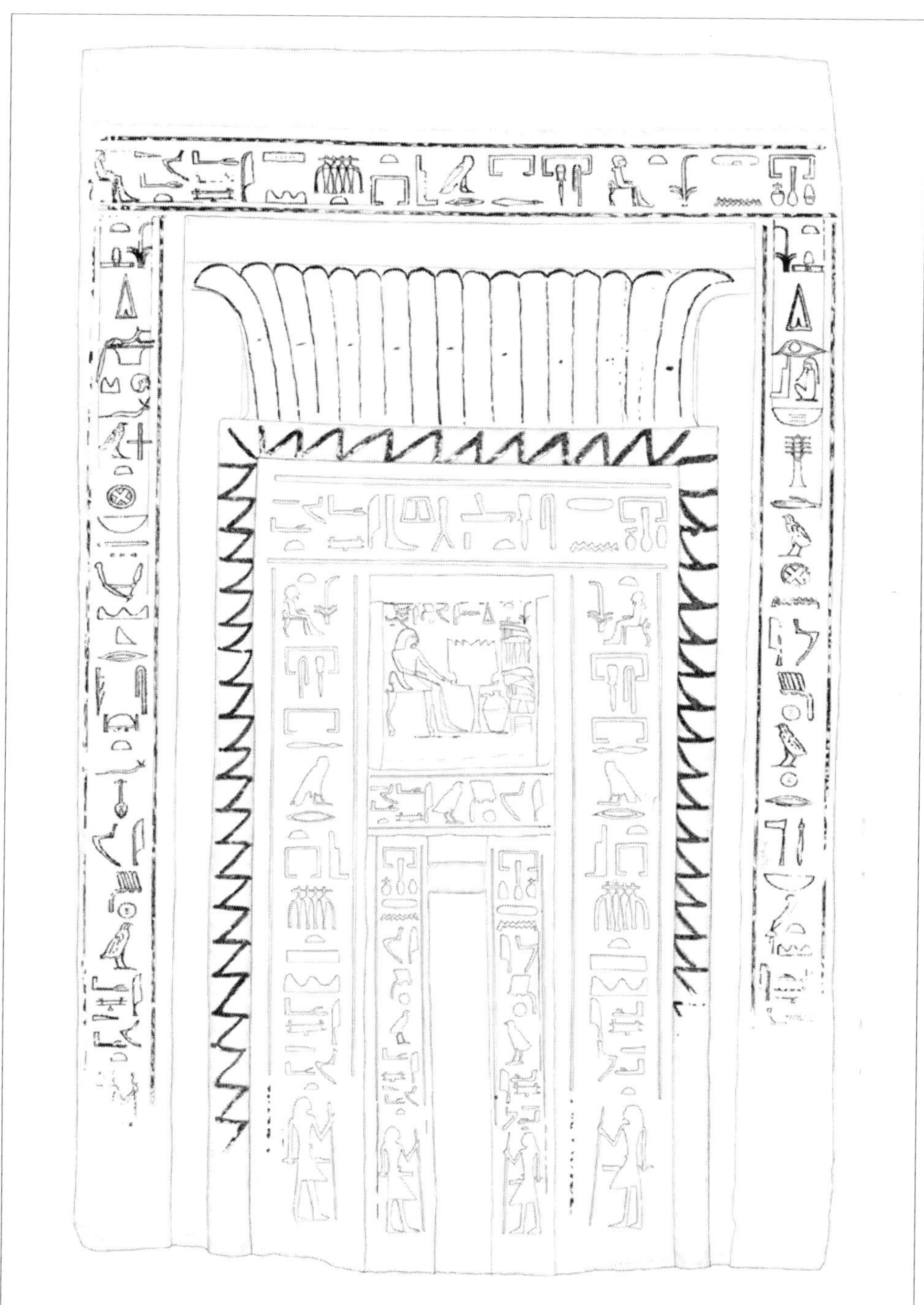

a
b
c
d

Fig. 23-24. Decoration of the southern wall of the chapel.

Fig. 25-26. Southern wall of the chapel – representation of Ia-Maat at the offering table.

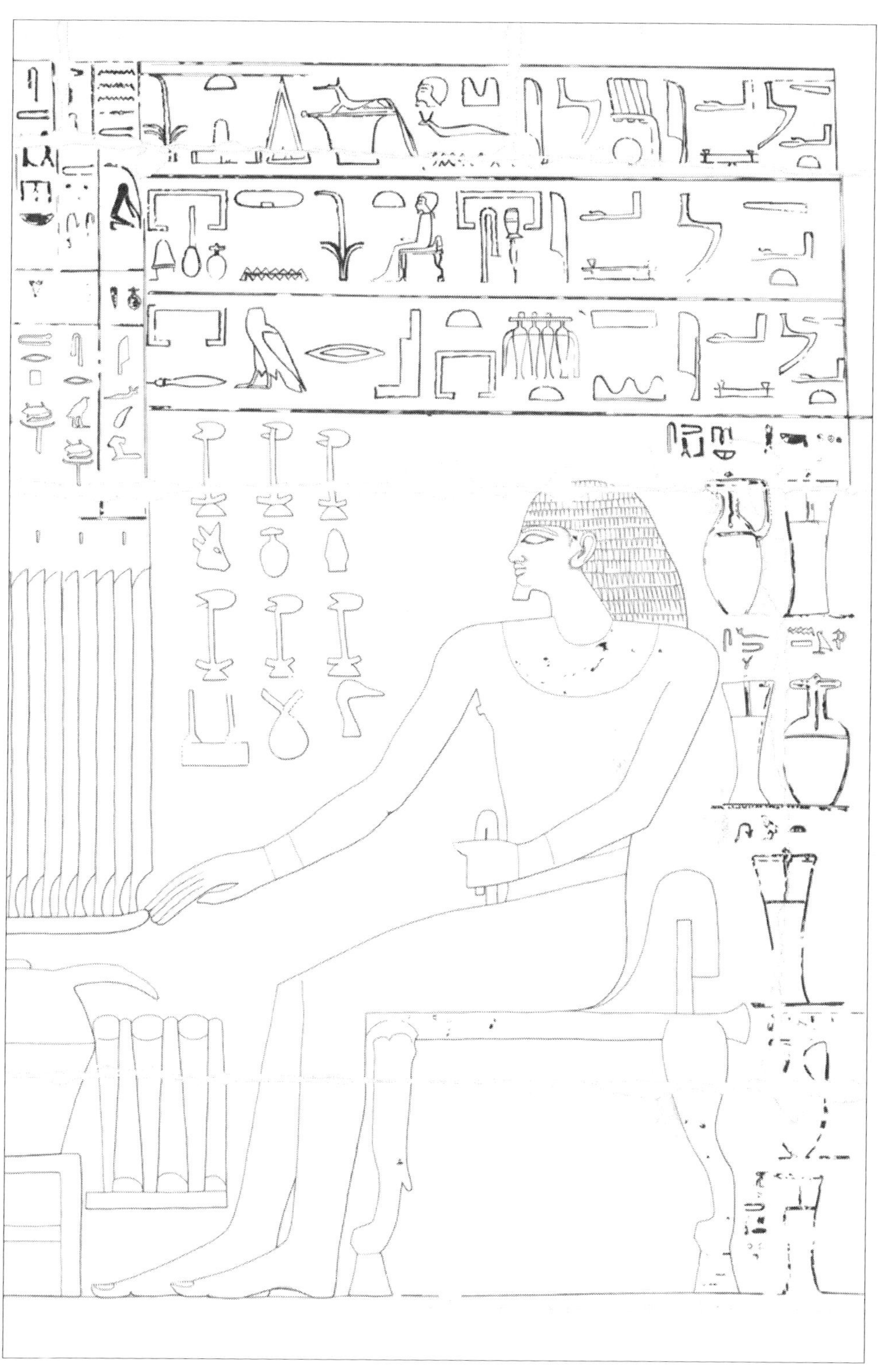

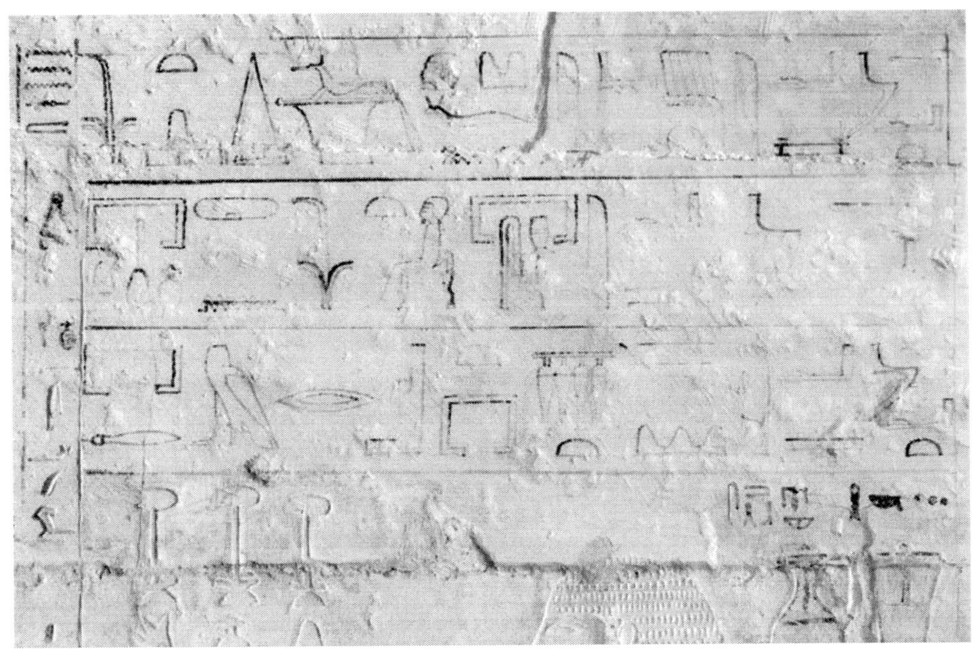

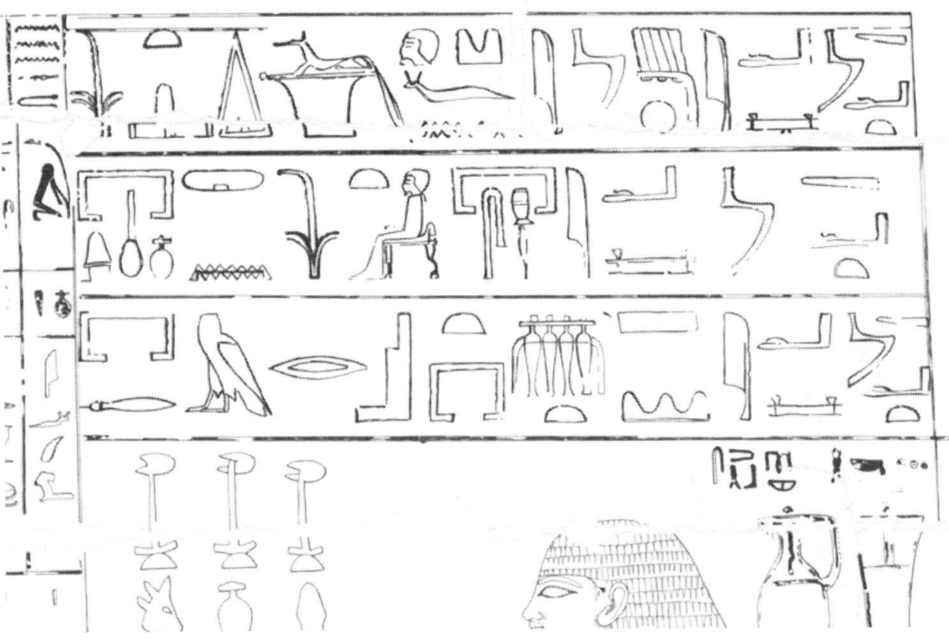

Fig. 27. Southern wall of the chapel – offering list, fragment a.

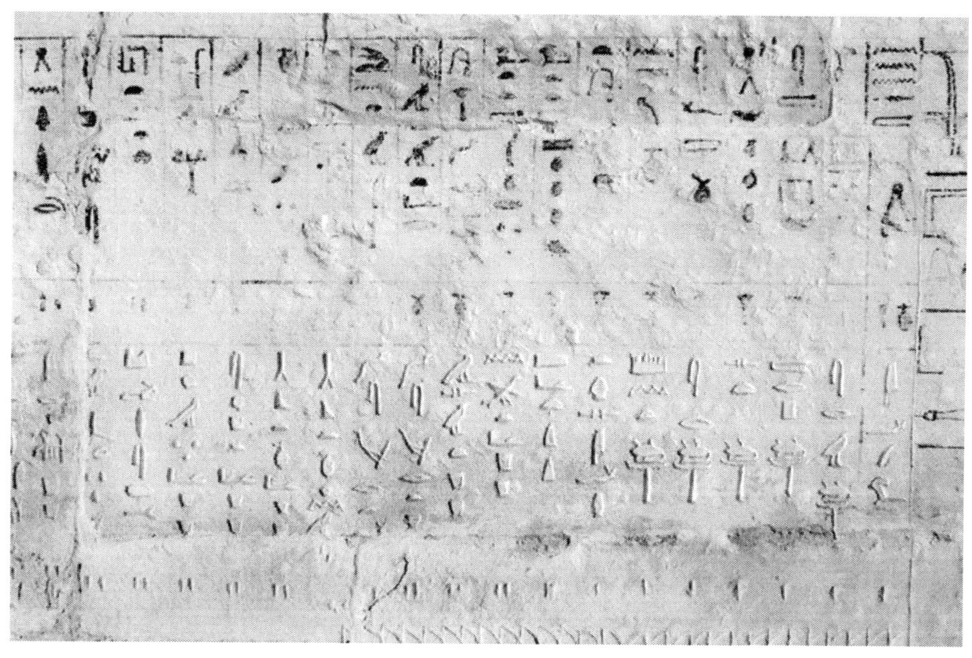

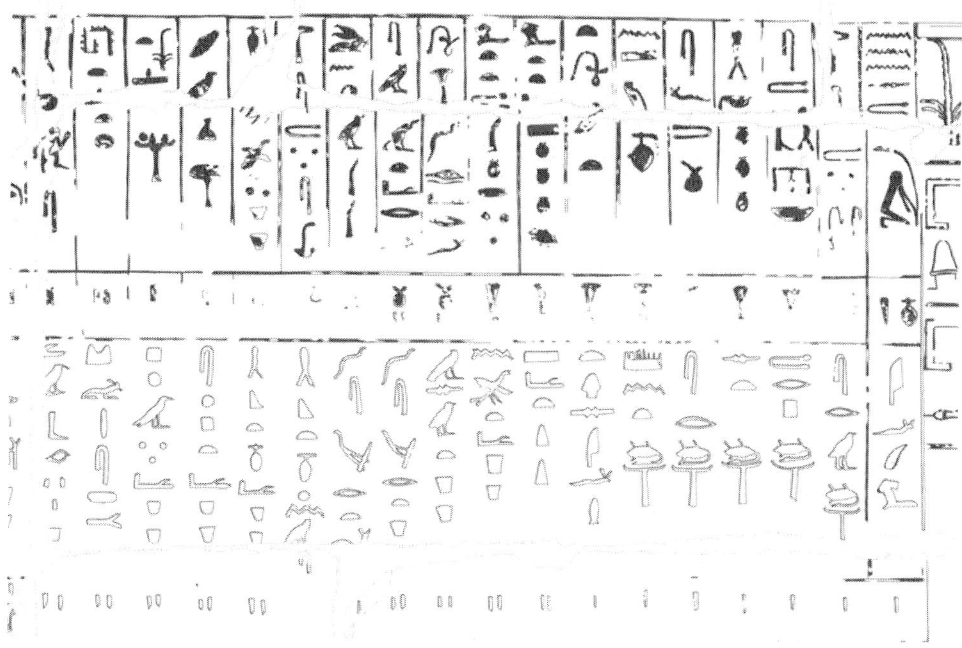

Fig. 28. Southern wall of the chapel – offering list, fragment b.

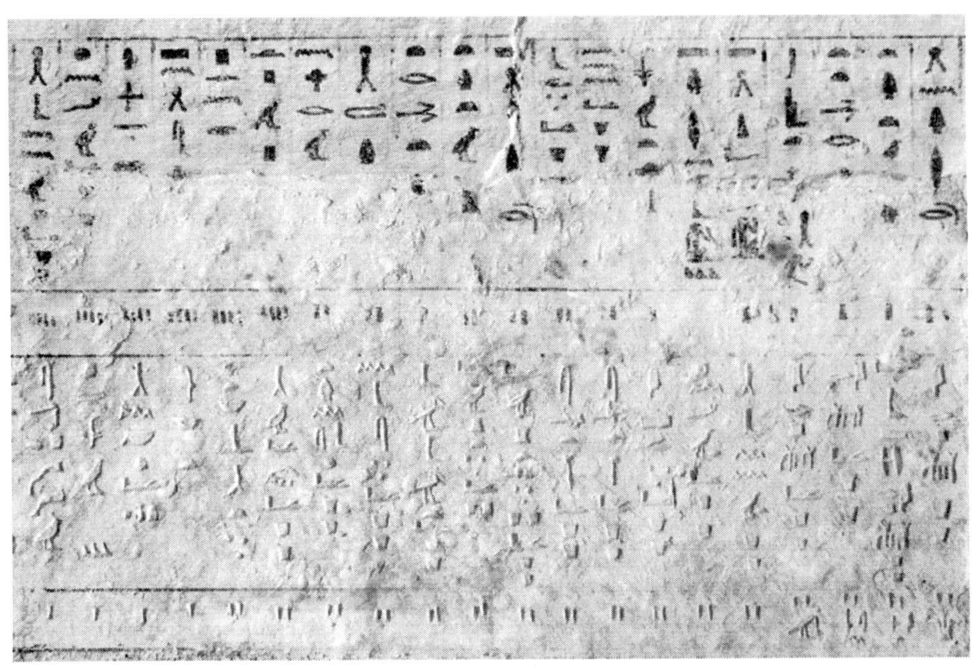

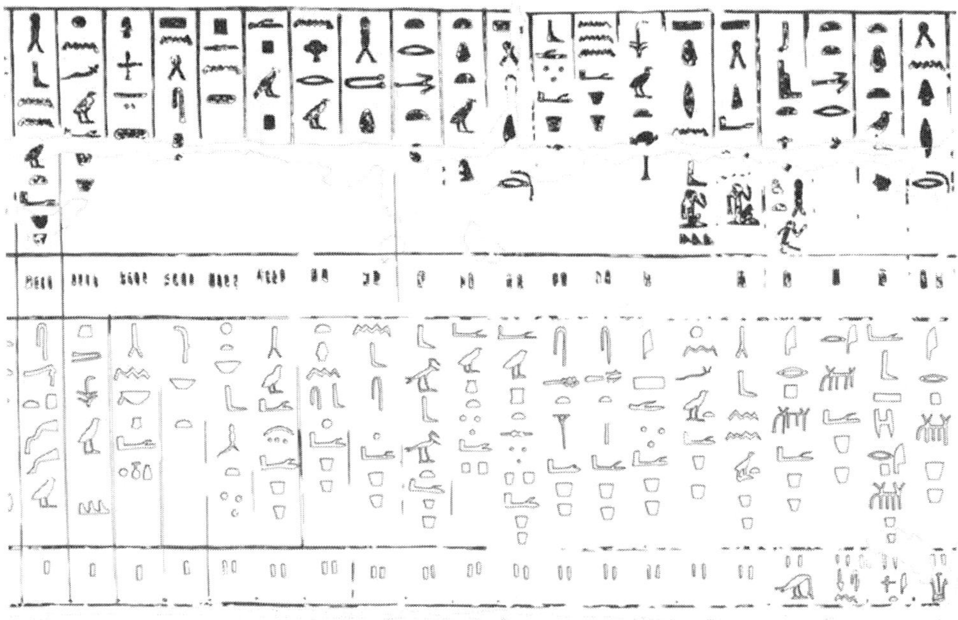

Fig. 29. Southern wall of the chapel – offering list, fragment c.

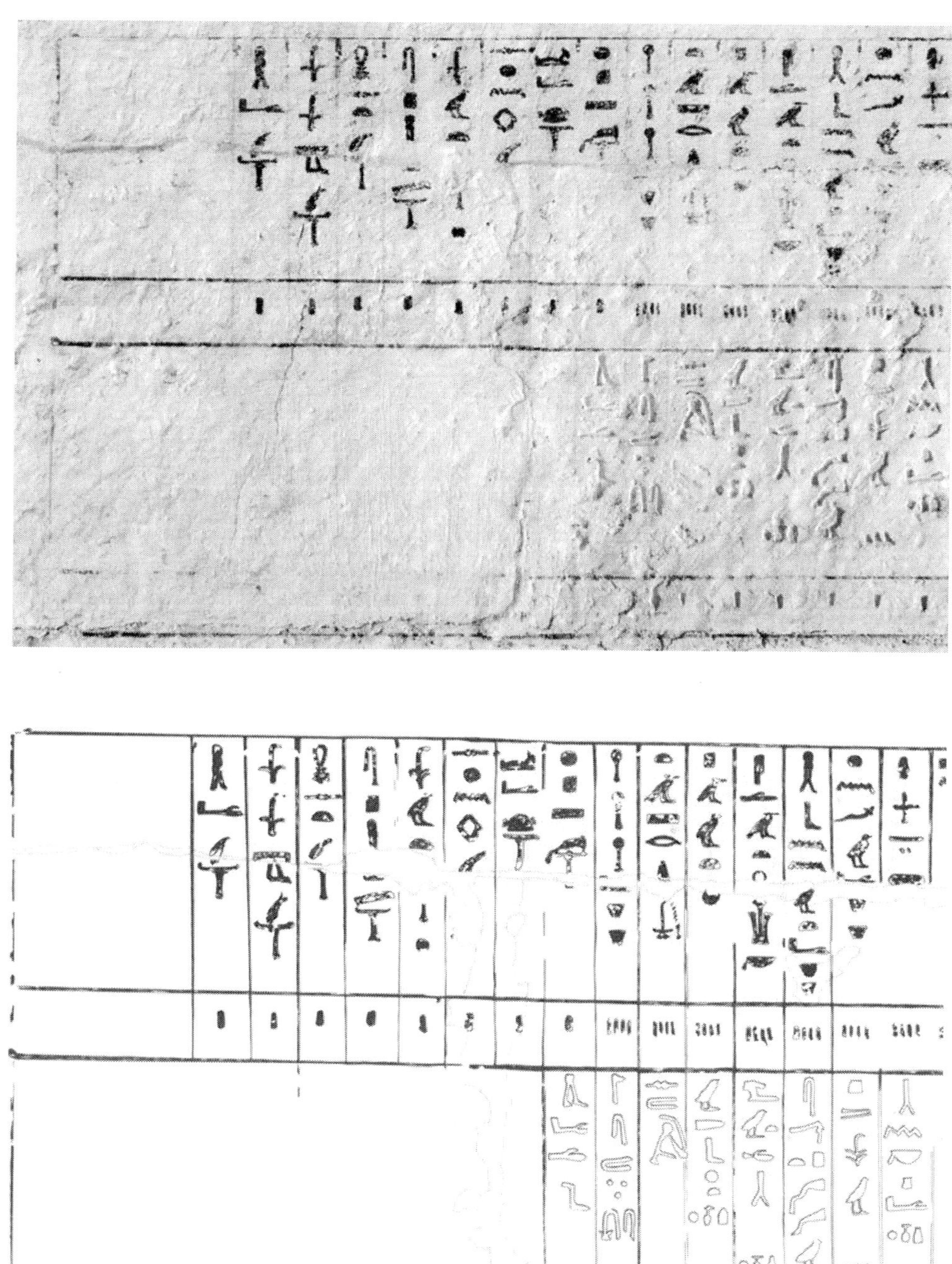

Fig. 30. Southern wall of the chapel – offering list, fragment d.

Fig. 31. Southern wall of the chapel – representation of Ia-Maat at the offering table.

Fig. 32. Detail of the above.

Fig. 33. The burial shaft seen from above.

Fig. 34. Embedded sarcophagus in the burial chamber.

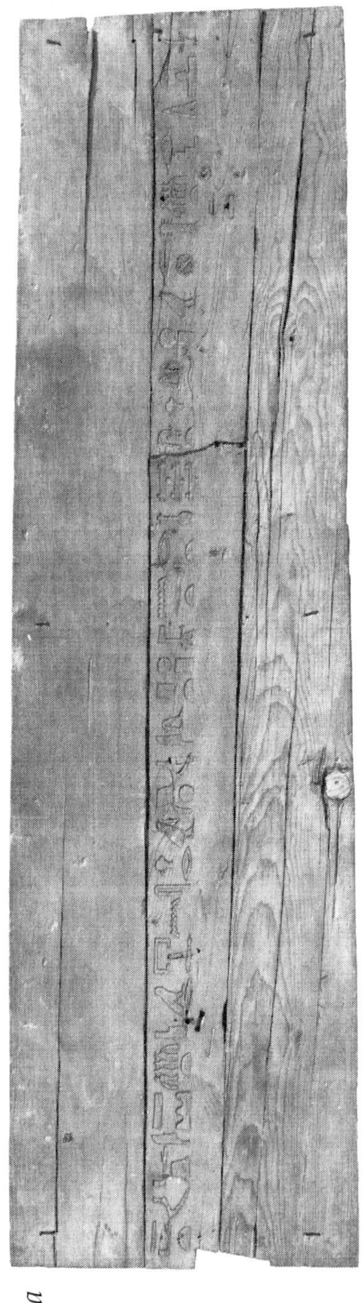

a

c

b

d

e

Fig. 35-36. Coffin of Ia-Maat – a) lid; b) northern side; c) southern side; d) western side; e) eastern side.

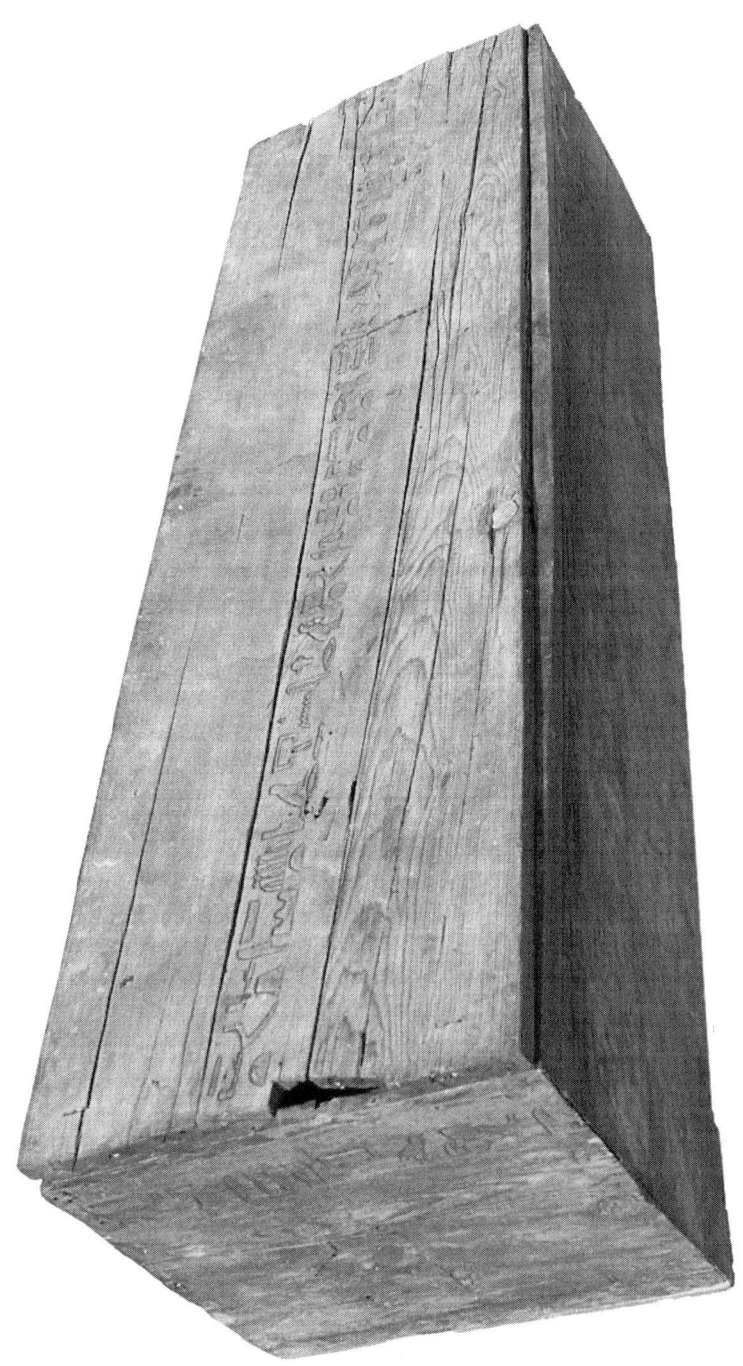

Fig. 37. The wooden coffin of Ia-Maat.

Fig. 38-39. Coffin: details of the eastern side.